614

DATE DUE

DEMCO 38-297

1997-98 NWMS READING BOOKS

RESOURCE BOOK FOR THE LEADER

IMAGINE THE POSSIBILITIES
Edited by Beverlee Borbe

FOR THE READER

BY GRACE TRANSFORMED
God at Work in Brazil
By Tim Crutcher

ONLY ONE LIFE . . .
The Autobiography of Lorraine O. Schultz
By Lorraine O. Schultz with C. Ellen Watts

JESUS WILL REPAY
By Becky Hancock

THAILAND: LAND OF THE WHITE ELEPHANT
Edited by Jean R. Knox and Michael P. McCarty

TO THE SHELTER
Journeys of Faith in the Middle East
By Kay Browning

WHERE THE RIVER FLOWS
Bringing Life to West Africa
By Linda Seaman

Jesus Will Repay

Becky Hancock

Nazarene Publishing House
Kansas City, Missouri

Copyright 1997
by Nazarene Publishing House

ISBN 083-411-6405

Printed in the
United States of America

Cover Design: Paul Franitza

All Scripture quotations not otherwise designated are from the *Holy Bible, New International Version*® (NIV®). Copyright © 1973, 1978, 1984 by International Bible Society. Used by permission of Zondervan Publishing House. All rights reserved.

10 9 8 7 6 5 4 3 2 1

This book is lovingly dedicated
to the memory of my daddy,
Marvin Ray Beam,
who is best described in Psalm 112:
"Blessed is the man who fears the LORD,
who finds great delight in his commands.
His children will be mighty in the land;
the generation of the upright will be blessed.
Wealth and riches are in his house,
and his righteousness endures forever. . . .
Good will come to him
who is generous and lends freely,
who conducts his affairs with justice.
Surely he will never be shaken;
a righteous man will be remembered forever" (vv. 1-6).

Contents

Introduction	9
1. Nothing Can Separate Us	11
2. Like Cold Water to a Weary Soul	18
3. If I Settle on the Far Side of the Sea	27
4. The Lord Will Watch Over Your Coming and Going	43
5. Strangers on Earth . . .	51
6. Whatever Your Hand Finds to Do	63
7. Whoever Does the Will of My Father . . .	78
Epilogue	92

Becky Hancock is a freelance writer, pastor's wife, piano teacher, and mother who has always had an interest in missions. She lives with her family in Goodlettsville, Tennessee. This is Becky's first book.

Introduction

I had been asked to sing a solo for a Wednesday evening missionary service. The song had already been selected for me—"O Zion, Haste." I knew the song slightly but didn't consider it to be one that would stir much emotion in me or in the congregation. But there I was, singing the third verse with a shaky voice, fighting the tears (I never have been able to sing and cry at the same time):

Give of thy sons to bear the message glorious.
  Give of thy wealth to speed them on their way.
Pour out thy soul for them in prayer victorious
  And all thou spendest, Jesus will repay.

I probably had sung those words before but not since my sister had become a missionary. It had a whole new meaning now. I felt our family had given a daughter and a sister, that we had given many dollars to our local churches in support of the lifeline of missions, that we had poured out many prayers for them already.

It was 1985, the beginning of the Radcliffe family's first term of service in Papua New Guinea, and Kathy Radcliffe is my sister. It was a dream come true for them and for us. We had known for many years this day would come, but we had no idea what radical changes it would bring to our lives. One really expects changes for the missionaries themselves—culture shock, a new language, new foods, and the like—but no one says much about how it affects the extended family of parents, grandparents, siblings, nieces and nephews, aunts and uncles, and in-laws.

The Radcliffe Family *(top row):* **Ben, Dr. Jim, and Kathy;** *(second row)* **Tim, Rebekah, Josiah, and Priscilla.**

Too often, perhaps, our emotions center on the pain of the separation. I am convinced that the last line of the song is more appropriate for our focus. Jesus has more than repaid us for the "spending" we have done. We have received much more than we have given. He has enriched our lives beyond all that we could ever ask or imagine. I want to share those blessings with you, the ones who have lovingly supported our Nazarene missionaries. Because of your prayers, interest, and financial generosity, our story is also your story.

1

Nothing Can Separate Us

THE OPPOSITE SIDE of the globe is a long way off! When I think about the 9,000 miles between my sister Kathy and me, it is hard to comprehend such a distance.

In June of 1985 our entire family attended the General Assembly of the Church of the Nazarene in Anaheim, California. The Radcliffes were departing at the close of the assembly for their first term as missionaries to Papua New Guinea (PNG).

Every moment was precious as we spent those busy days with thousands of fellow Nazarenes. I remember hoping for a few private moments with Kathy before she left. We did have one afternoon together beside the motel pool, where I got a chance to talk with her alone.

I remember her saying that one of her fears was that people would forget about them—the old "out of sight, out of mind" principle. She feared that the longer they were gone, the less contact would be maintained and that eventually many relationships would be lost. I was surprised by her fear because I was so confident that many loving people would continue to care just as much about their work after they left as they had during their months of preparation.

Realistically, I know that it is the norm for contact to be more frequent during the first part of any separation. The 12 years that the Radcliffes have served as missionaries have proven that the phone calls, audiotapes, videotapes, and letters do tend to slow down. But as a loyal sister I was convinced that I would be faithful to keep in touch even if no one else was.

Jim and Kathy both experienced their calls to full-time missionary service very early in life. Kathy recalls her heart being especially moved by reading junior missionary books as a child. Jim answered his call during a Nazarene youth camp and shared it publicly. Since their romance had begun during their freshman year of high school, Kathy decided to keep God's plan for her life a secret for a little while, lest her intentions be misunderstood. Kathy finally testified about her call to missions during her sophomore year of high school.

After eight years of friendship, dating, and courtship through high school and college, Jim and Kathy were married in June of 1976. Jim had graduated from Mount Vernon Nazarene College (MVNC) with a premed degree that spring. Kathy had transferred from MVNC after her sophomore year, and she received her degree in medical dietetics from Ohio State University.

Jim's acceptance into medical school at Ohio State was a major achievement for him and for MVNC, since Jim was in MVNC's first class to earn bachelor's degrees. The family prayed about his applications and knew his first choice was Ohio State, and the Lord worked a miracle in giving him the desire of his heart.

The Radcliffes spent eight years in Columbus, Ohio, while Jim completed medical school and his residency in general surgery. Two children were born during those years of training—Benjamin in 1980 and Rebekah in 1983. (I have always said we sisters have a "mutual admiration society," since she named her daughter Rebekah, and I named my daughter Katherine.) One year as an associate in an established surgical practice in our hometown of Xenia, Ohio, and Jim's medical preparation was complete. During that year, they also spoke in deputation services to raise money for their vehicle. God enabled them to pay their debts, sell their home, and even make a contribution to faith promise.

So the big "send-off" in 1985 was an event that had been long anticipated in the lives of Jim and Kathy and their families. General Assembly came to an end, and emotions ran high as we gathered at the Los Angeles International airport. Kathy wrote about it later:

> The time at the L.A. airport was sweet. There were very few other people around since our flight was at 11 P.M. We sang "Blessed Assurance" and "One Flock, One Shepherd," standing in a circle with family and friends. They had prayer for us; then through our tears, we hugged everyone and headed for the plane. We had not expected our leaving to be so hard, for we had planned to be missionaries for most

of our lives. It was the fulfillment of our dreams and many years of preparation. Putting into action our yes to God's calling for our lives was a big step.

I will never forget one lump after another forming in my throat during our last hour together as I watched others getting their last turn at a conversation and their final hug. The two Radcliffe children (ages four and two) and two of their cousins (my children, ages six and three) were protected by their youthful innocence. They could not possibly comprehend how long four years would be or how many miles would separate them from each other. So they just playfully romped around in that spacious airport waiting area.

In the midst of all the tears my three-year-old daughter, Katherine, queried, "Mommy, can I cry too?" My emotions were intense since I was five months pregnant, and I wondered if Kathy would have the opportunity to see my baby before he was four years old. I still get misty-eyed when I remember the burst of pent-up emotion that came forth in hard sobs as my turn came for the final good-bye embrace.

No, it isn't easy to allow precious loved ones to go far away, even when letting them go to do God's work. But that doesn't mean one is unwilling to give them. We were all supportive of this decision. The Radcliffes' first newsletter reflects these simultaneous emotions of sadness and peace that come with painful obedience: "Despite our tears, there was a definite awareness of the support of our family and loved ones in our desire to follow God's leading."

Several weeks after the Radcliffes arrived in PNG, I was still dealing with the stages of grief and the process of adjustment. I began to understand the common description of a "wave of grief" when I experienced this separation from my sister. Often it was embarrassing to be sharing bits of news and information from the Radcliffes with interested friends when a wave of sadness would flood over me and I could not control the tears.

These strong emotions diminish slightly as time heals the hurt of separation. But at times a simple thought can still trigger a family memory and bring the emotion to the surface in an instant.

With our limited direct contact or physical closeness, we have learned the importance of "being there" in prayer. Realizing that this is even better than our physical presence has been a real lesson in faith to us. Our prayers usually are much more powerful than our own ability to do something for our family on the other side of the world. A song by Morris Chapman became very special to us in those early days. It says:

I may not always be there to take you by the hand.
I may not always be there to listen or understand.
I may not always be there when life seems all uphill,
But I know Someone who always will!

I may not always be there to hear you when you cry.
I may not always be there to wipe a tear from your eye.
I may not always be at your bedside all the time
   when you're feeling ill,
But I know Someone who always will.

> *Jesus will always be there. He knows how much I
> love you.*
> *And in ev'ry situation He'll be there to see you
> through.*
> *I may not always be there, but let your heart be
> peaceful and still.*
> *I know Someone who always will . . . His name is
> Jesus.**

I have always loved to browse in card shops. Only a few times in my life had I found a reason for looking at the "Missing You" section of greeting cards. That first year after Kathy left for PNG, it seemed I always chose to look there first, and I bought many special cards to express my feelings to her. It was difficult to express our true emotions to our loved ones serving far away without wondering if we were causing homesickness that could be an unhealthy burden to them as new missionaries.

One day during the Radcliffes' first term as missionaries, as I read the familiar verse in Romans 8:39, the Lord allowed me to have a fresh insight into this precious passage. The Word says that nothing ". . . will be able to separate us from the love of God that is in Christ Jesus our Lord."

I began to apply this truth horizontally as well as vertically. If nothing separates me from God's love and nothing separates Kathy from God's love

---

*"I May Not Always Be There," by Morris Chapman, Niles Borop. © 1984 Word Music (A Division of Word Entertainment, Inc.). All rights reserved. Used by permission.

even while she is in PNG, then we have a very direct connection with each other as we are living in His love. It helped me to think that we were not really separated at all, that the geographical distance was insignificant when compared to the intimacy we had in Christ Jesus. Time after time God's Word has held meaningful promises for us as we have learned to give our fears or pain to the Lord.

2

Like Cold Water to a Weary Soul

NOW THAT WE WERE spending much of our energy and time in getting news from the other side of the world, we kept saying how thankful we all were that we lived in the technological age. Our attitude toward separation and our methods of communication would have been completely different a generation ago. Our veteran missionaries remember the days when the only contact with home was a letter that would arrive two to four weeks after it was written. Telephones were unavailable or too expensive. When a family member went to the field then, there was much more of a sense of separation than there is today.

Soon after the Radcliffes' arrival in PNG, they discovered this precious verse in Proverbs 25:25: "Like cold water to a weary soul is good news from a distant land." We have found that news from the other side of the world is the most exciting mail we receive. When a letter arrives, I am eager to "take a drink" of the good news immediately. It's always a highlight of my day to devour that "cold water" as soon as it arrives and then, later, to read it over several times.

During their deputation travels before leaving for the mission field, the Radcliffes had been given a video camcorder. Within six months all of us stateside families had bought VCRs and cameras so we could send video news back and forth.

Through the miracle of video we have traveled the rough roads of the bush country and watched our missionaries build makeshift bridges to cross the streams. We have attended services and witnessed the enthusiastic singing and hand-clapping of the Papua New Guineans as they worship in their own churches. We have "scrubbed in" and donned surgical masks and gowns to observe Dr. Jim at work in the operating room. We were there when the third, fourth, and fifth Radcliffe children were born in the Nazarene hospital at Kudjip, and we have watched while birthday and Christmas presents that we sent were opened in their living room.

Just as we have shared their lives, our missionary family has been able to share ours. They have experienced several holiday musical productions of our local churches here in the United States. The Radcliffes have attended piano recitals, concerts, weddings, and even funeral services through the eye of the video camera.

In those early days whenever a video arrived from PNG, a few copies were made and eventually distributed to several family members. Our appetite for current news from PNG was voracious.

Jim's mother, Helen Radcliffe, and Kathy's and my mother, Garnet Beam, were especially eager when they knew one had received a videotape and the other had to wait a few days until her copy arrived.

In addition to videotapes, we planned a rotation for our telephone calls so that a different sibling or parent would call PNG each week. We thought a weekly telephone visit with the Radcliffes during the first few months would be a help to all of us in dealing with our adjustments to this separation. Whoever made the call would then attempt to communicate the news to the rest of the family here.

The advent of audiocassette tapes was no doubt a blessing to those on the mission field in the late 1960s so that one could actually hear the voice of a loved one. Although we had the video technology when the Radcliffes began their missionary service in 1985, we still occasionally exchanged hour-long "chats" on audiotape. The listener could enjoy a lot of news while involved in other tasks, such as washing dishes or cleaning house. Audiotapes were great for capturing the routine sounds of family life or little voices learning to talk or sing or recite. When we had too long a list of things to cover in a letter or when we wanted to just express ourselves conversationally, the audiotape was ideal.

Those who have served on Nazarene fields for three or four decades might say today's new missionaries "have it made." Now that facsimile transmission machines, or faxes, are available, we can have instant letters.

I well remember the first fax that I sent to PNG. A fax machine had been installed at the hospital on the mission station at Kudjip in 1991. At home we did not have convenient access to a fax machine, so during the General Assembly in Indianapolis in 1993 our family impulsively sent one from the front desk of the hotel.

Our denomination's quadrennial conference has been a family event for all of us since 1968, but the 1993 convention was our first General Assembly without the Radcliffes. I was particularly homesick for them one night, and I was disappointed that they were missing the inspiration, challenge, fellowship, and family times that we were all enjoying.

That evening as all the Beam family was gathered in one hotel room, we suddenly remembered it was Priscilla Radcliffe's first birthday. Calculating the time difference, we realized that we could send a fax immediately and it would actually arrive as a surprise birthday greeting. It was exciting to pass around that paper for all the grandparents, aunts, uncles, and cousins to write notes and messages.

As we worked on it, someone suggested we draw pictures for the birthday baby. I was shocked! I had assumed a fax was similar to a telegram and only the words would be printed out on the other end. They had to explain to me that a fax is an exact reproduction of what one sends. (Welcome to the information highway, Becky!)

I was like a child with a new toy as I took that letter so lovingly prepared to the front desk and excitedly watched as they sent it through. It was thrilling to know that our birthday greeting from General Assembly would be in the Radcliffes' hands in a matter of minutes. These technologies make it seem like our loved ones are much closer than halfway around the world.

Now our local church offices have fax machines available, and we are enjoying more frequent fax communication. Our church purchased one during the Radcliffes' furlough in 1995, so after they returned to the mission field it occurred to me that we could try this new way of keeping in touch. Not only was sending one very memorable, but receiving my first fax at the church was quite exciting.

I had just taken my seat for Wednesday evening service when my husband walked up and handed me a freshly faxed letter from PNG that he had discovered in the fax machine. I was so proud as I shared this prized possession with our church folks that night. One of our precious "golden agers" (90 years young) was especially fascinated by this 20th-century technology and how it really worked. We can normally send a one-page fax for the cost of a one- to two-minute phone call.

One Sunday evening in December of 1995 our son Nathan was in the church office after the service and noticed a recent letter still in the fax machine tray. He was thrilled to see that it was a correspondence from the Radcliffes that had just arrived moments before. It read:

> This is from Jim for you to share/send to

the rest of the family: I have lost weight and Kathy has gained some. One reason for this is that we are joyfully expecting our fifth child. This is not an accident nor a surprise for us however. We have been prayerfully open to the possibility that God would bless us with the privilege of raising another life for His glory and service. We have just told the children tonight. Some say children keep us young. I hope this will be true and perhaps it will work for grandparents, uncles, aunts, and cousins too! Ha! Please feel free to come and see the baby—due date June 26.

In May of 1996 the latest in technology came to Kudjip as Field Director Vern Ward set up his office computer with E-mail. This service is only as efficient as the phone service in PNG, which is sometimes unpredictable in its availability. Now that our families are connected with E-mail services, we are looking forward to exploring the possibilities of using this new means of communication. We are already finding it to be a fast and inexpensive means of correspondence.

Despite all this technology, we have found that the old-fashioned way of communicating through a letter is very important to missionaries. Receiving mail from home is especially crucial for the new missionary. The Radcliffes have seen noticeable contrasts between those who have supportive families who keep in touch regularly and those who do not. It is especially painful for those whose families object to their decision to leave the comforts of home to fulfill their calling to missions. Any personal mail from home is a real boost to each missionary. One has really given a part of himself when he takes the time to pen some words of encouragement and news from home to those whom we've sent to other countries.

Our frequency of letter writing has slowed down considerably since those first months, but that has been understandable and practical for all of us. We have found that the "family letter" is the best way for them to answer us. Kathy writes one letter on the computer, makes multiple copies, and sends one to each family. This method gives us all the latest news about their general activities, and usually a personal note is handwritten to each recipient at the end.

Missionaries are always grateful for letters received, but the correspondence expectations can be very overwhelming. The ability to keep up with answering every piece of correspondence quickly becomes impractical for a missionary. In one of Kathy's family letters she succinctly communicated that limitation by saying, "I wish all of our thoughts and conversations of you could be automatic letters. You would be getting lots of mail!" For this reason many missionaries produce a newsletter.

When Jim and Kathy first went to PNG, there were 600 on their mailing list, and they wrote a newsletter every three to four months. As the years have passed the mailing list has grown to nearly 1,000, and the amount of time available for correspondence has diminished. So now they send one every 6 to 12 months.

Like many missionaries, the Radcliffes compose and fax their newsletter information to people in their home country. In our case that means Kathy's and my family in Ohio. The Beams are responsible to get the newsletter copied at a local print shop and mailed as soon as possible. There are numerous faithful folks who invest many hours and subsidize the expense of newsletter production for scores of Nazarene missionaries. Hats off to you who donate this labor of love! We pay special tribute to those who graciously do this for the Radcliffes: Nancy Casserta of Edwards Printing Company, Dave Beam, Mom Beam, and the helpful office and pastoral staff of the Xenia First Church of the Nazarene.

Last, but certainly not least, on the communication list come packages. Surface mail takes two to six months from the United States to PNG, so it is difficult to predict the arrival time of a package sent the "cheap" way. This means that missionaries often get to celebrate several Christmases each year. Smaller, lightweight packages can be airmailed and arrive in about two weeks.

I sometimes find myself shopping for gifts with size and weight in mind. Books and other heavy or large items aren't as likely to be sent as small things like audiotapes, socks, barrettes, jewelry, pens, pencils, and wallets. Occasionally, the postage for some gifts may be more expensive than the gifts themselves.

Often LINKS districts will ask us about the special needs and requests of our missionary family. *L*oving, *I*nterested *N*azarenes have *K*nown and *S*hared specific items that cannot be found unless they are sent from the United States. These and all the other surprise packages find many uses as they are opened. Often they are shared with other missionaries and nationals on the station who can benefit from these gifts. God bless those who have prepared and mailed packages to our missionaries in other countries!

Some of the best "gifts" we at home have received are from our fellow Nazarenes who care about the Radcliffes enough to ask questions about them, listen to us talk about them, and then intercede on their behalf. I am always aware that not everyone wants to hear all the details—almost as if we are asking them to watch our home movies.

We have become sensitive to the fact that we might "bore" some people if we go on too long talking about a subject that is so dear to our hearts but removed from theirs. When we find someone who knows about the Radcliffes' ministry and has questions, it is easy to keep that conversation going. Of course, when we find willing listeners, we are eager to share because people cannot genuinely care unless they are adequately informed.

3

If I Settle on the Far Side of the Sea

FROM WHERE I LIVE, PNG is certainly on the "far side of the sea," clear across the Pacific Ocean. I find great comfort in the psalmist's words in Psalm 139. "Where can I go from your Spirit? Where can I flee from your presence? . . . if I settle on the far side of the sea, even there your hand will guide me, your right hand will hold me fast" (verses 7, 9b-10). This gives me assurance that God's hand is with the Radcliffes, although they have settled on the far side of the Pacific Ocean, away from all that is familiar to them.

Many people have to locate Papua New Guinea in relation to the continent of Australia, because Australia is more prominent geographically. New Guinea is the dinosaur-shaped island just north of Australia. The country of Papua New Guinea consists of the eastern half of New Guinea, the second largest island in the world. A chain of tropical islands off the eastern coast of the larger island is also included as PNG territory.

Being close to the equator creates a hot, humid climate in PNG, but many mountainous areas called "highlands" have moderate temperatures. With a continuous growing season, the term "perpetual spring" describes the appealing nature of the weather in the highlands. The rainy season is the only inconvenience, making rubber boots a necessary part of one's footwear.

For most of the 20th century PNG was under the control of Australia. In 1975 PNG gained its independence and is now struggling to establish itself with the rapid changes that have occurred in the ensuing years. Because of the high mountains in the interior, many of the rural villages were totally isolated from the outside world until this century. Culturally, the Melanesian people from this country have needed a "crash course in the 20th century" as they have become acquainted with the rest of the world.

A new thrust of mission health-care work is the emphasis upon community-based health promotion, which involves helping the villages identify their own problems. They are taught the basics of sanitation, hygiene, nutrition, and health care. They are also discipled spiritually and taught to minister themselves, instead of relying on outside help and health-care institutions.

The church has seen dramatic results with this new approach: reduction of preventable illness, a feeling of national ownership, souls being won to God, and encouraging church growth. Missionary nurse Evelyn Wiens initiated a program of this kind in 1993 in PNG. Carolyn Myatt, along with several national health workers, is now in charge of this work, which has previously been successful in Africa and India. It is hoped that community-based health care will spread to every part of the work in PNG.

Malnutrition is not as common in PNG as in other developing countries since the climate allows farming to be so productive. Most families have gardens full of vegetables. Oranges, pineapples, and bananas grow in abundance. Agriculture is the basis of most of the economy, and the sweet potato or *kaukau* [cow-cow] is the staple food of their diet. During my visit to our Nazarene hospital in the village of Kudjip, I was fascinated to observe the method of hospital food service delivery to patients—a wheelbarrow full of *kau-kau!* Any additional food must be supplied by the family of the patient.

The traditional feast or banquet in PNG is called a *mumu* [moo-moo]. They dig a large pit in the ground and fill it with hot rocks. The food is then placed in the pit, which has been lined and covered with banana leaves, and left to steam for several hours. The menu consists of greens, potatoes, cooking bananas, corn, cabbage, and meat (lamb, chicken, or pork) combined to make one big "pot" of food. The meal is then served on a banana leaf in place of a plate and eaten with the fingers—messy, but delicious! I was privileged to attend a *mumu* after a baptismal service during my visit. The corn and bananas were different from what I was used to, but the cabbage and lamb were delicious. I was thankful for the fork and plate that the Radcliffes provided, and it was definitely the most interesting picnic I have ever attended.

One of the most interesting cultural characteristics of PNG is its language. Because of the rugged mountains preventing contact among the tribes, there are approximately 800 tribal languages in the country. To communicate with each other and with "white men" who came into their areas, the people use a trade language based on English called Pidgin English *(Tok Pisin)*.

Despite its limited vocabulary, Pidgin is quite necessary for communication throughout PNG. The official language is English, but since the educational system has not been available to all, many adults remain illiterate. Many of our Nazarene worship services are conducted in Pidgin, and all of the Bible has been translated into Pidgin. The New Testament was first published in 1969, and the entire Bible became available in 1989.

This colorful language is fascinating to compare to English. The pronunciation is very simplistic and phonetic. *"Mi gat sik"* is "I am sick." To do something quickly is *"hariap"* or *"kwiktaim,"* which could be easily associated with our phrase "hurry up" or the phrase "quick time." I have a plaque that says, *"prea oltaim,"* which means "pray always" or "pray all the time." The word for "Lord" in Pidgin is *Bikpela,* which relates to our words "big fellow." The language of Pidgin English is what our missionaries learn and use to communicate with most of the Papua New Guineans.

One of my gifts from the Radcliffes is a hymnal in Tok Pisin. It was published in 1985 with parallel translations of each song in Pidgin English and standard English included. I enjoy comparing the two languages to see if I can determine the origin of the Pidgin phrases from English.

The rest of the languages, the tribal languages, are called *Tok Ples* (the talk of the place), and occasionally a missionary will attempt to also learn the specific language of a local tribe. These languages are more intimately expressive of the culture of the people. Because of this, Bible translations in the local languages are most desirable. It is much more time-consuming and difficult to learn the local languages than to learn Pidgin, but many of the older Papua New Guineans still do not relate to the Pidgin English Bible translation.

The work to be done by Bible translators in PNG is monumental. New Tribes Mission and Wycliffe missionaries have a tremendous ministry in PNG. Portions of the New Testament have been translated into many of these tribal languages. The full New Testament was published in the local Waghi Tok Ples (where the Nazarene hospital is located) in 1990. This work was done by the late Dr. Evelyn Ramsey and Rev. and Mrs. Bruce Blowers, all Nazarene missionaries.

Language barriers create an interesting environment for church services. Some worship only in Pidgin. Others use the Tok Ples and have it translated into Pidgin on occasions when several missionaries or others are present who cannot understand the local language. When a guest speaker is preaching in English, sometimes his message has to "turn talk twice" or be translated from English to Pidgin to Tok Ples.

At the beginning of the Radcliffes' second term in 1991, they had requested some special time away from the mission station to saturate themselves in the language and culture of a local tribe. Plans were made for them to build a bush home in Konduk. This village is just a 30-minute drive up a mountain road from the mission compound. This venture would allow the Radcliffe family to live among the national people and spend six months in concentrated study of the Kuma language.

The Radcliffes spent many months in preparation for this move, and we were excited for them. In September 1991 the Radcliffes wrote in their newsletter:

> It has been a lot of work to get ready and oversee the building of the house, but we are thankful for this opportunity. The people in the village have been very eager for us to come and live among them. We were reminded of an old-fashioned "barn raising" as all the people worked together on building the house and readying our garden. This will be an interesting adventure for our whole family. It has been good to see God at work in our local church family at Konduk.

This adventure became a source of both blessing and heartache within a short period of time. The village people were honored to have these mis-

The "bush house" at Konduk

sionaries learning their way of life, and the Radcliffes became an integral part of the Konduk Church of the Nazarene. Rebekah took on the responsibility of placing flowers around the church, since floral decorations usually grace the church buildings for weekly worship services in PNG. Jim and Kathy prepared their testimonies in *tok ples* and shared them with the congregation in slow, broken Kuma. Pastor Peter ate meals with them and helped with the language study.

Dr. Jim did language study in the morning while Kathy led the children in their regular school lessons. In the afternoons Kathy studied while the children worked and played with Dad. The language lessons were developed by Bruce and Ruth Blowers, Nazarene missionaries who were translating the New Testament into the Kuma language.

Jim and Kathy kept a memo book as they visited with the villagers each day. One time Kathy exclaimed, "How the people loved to help us!"

All these experiences helped the Radcliffes have a deeper understanding of the Papua New Guinean culture. But this enriching venture was cut short and interrupted unexpectedly. After just one month of being in their bush home, Jim and Kathy's plans were changed. We shared their turmoil when we received this newsletter in February 1992:

> October 1 was the beginning of the heaviness and disruptions that changed our plans and lives drastically. Just minutes after we passed through Kudjip village that day on our way back to Konduk, a fight with sticks, stones, and axes broke out. There had been a court settling land disputes and compensation for a small fight, but everyone, evidently, was not happy with the outcome. The two enemy ("brother") lines were the Konduk people and the Kudjip people, though they live intermixed all up and down the mountain. It was very different for us from any other fighting or disputes that have occurred in these 5½ years we have been in PNG. We understood and felt so much more because we lived at Konduk. The anger, unrest, and fear continued to the extent that our national Christian leaders advised us not to stay in our Konduk house after a second fight in which a man was killed. We were torn and heartbroken.

It was difficult to see our Christians being tested. We worshiped with the Konduk people on Sundays even though we were not living there. We missionaries gave them God's words on revenge . . . but our people seemed to be pulled into the plans for "payback." We cannot completely understand their extreme loyalty to clan, but the old ways prevailed, and three more deaths occurred in the weeks of fighting that followed. Houses were burned, coffee trees and gardens destroyed, and the Konduk people were driven from their land. Only the church, pastor's house, and our house remained at Konduk. We eventually moved all of our belongings from the house, for it was being looted. The Konduk people scattered over all of the Waghi Valley, living with relatives and friends of other tribes.

The short verse in Kuma that is a favorite of the Konduk people has become our promise as we pray for revival and peace: *"Got yap kanem kanem kaple ende, enda."* ("For nothing is impossible with God" [Luke 1:37].)

From the beginning, we had prayed for miracles, for a sweeping revival of the Christians, and for many nonbelievers to turn to the Lord. We have seen His hand as some have faced the death of their loved ones—Christians being called home to heaven has a way of getting minds on to eternal things. Others have turned to God as they have spent time in prison, accused of killing in the fight. The provincial secretary has invited the Church of the Nazarene to open a new church at his place because of the refugee Christians who have let their light shine as he allowed them to live on his land. One of the Konduk leaders who had cancer was staying at the secretary's place since the fight, and he received the Lord as his Savior, was baptized, and sent on to be with Jesus last week!

God's words are true: "Those who sow in tears will reap with songs of joy. He who goes out weeping, carrying seed to sow, will return with songs of joy, carrying sheaves with him" (Psalm 126:5-6). The songs of joy are beginning. The sheaves are being brought into the Kingdom. Those of you who have prayed, keep on praying. We believe the Konduk church will someday be a reality again, that the people will be able to return to their ground, and that the Lord will be glorified as people seek Him and peace is restored in our villages.

We must admit we have grieved over many things, including the money and time spent to build and furnish our language study house, especially when we think about many of you who gave in our deputation offerings to help build it. Due to continued vandalism we have taken down our house and given some of the salvaged materials for national housing here on the mission station. One of our missionary colleagues, Bruce Blowers, helped us take down our house. The next day he preached about the broken, spilled-out offering of perfume poured over Jesus. He said, "It may seem that your dreams were shattered, that the time and money were spent just to be spoiled; but give it to the Lord as an offering that can go out as sweet perfume for His glory." What encouragement we received from those words!

As we heard of the challenges that came to the Radcliffes during this unique cultural experience, we shared deeply in the pain and disappointment of the Papua New Guineans. We prayed often for these people who were being uprooted from their homes and shared in their joy as they reestablished their village and church.

From 1991 to the spring of 1994 there was continuous tension and occasional violent incidents between these two neighboring tribes. The Radcliffes were preparing for their furlough in June of 1994 and had prayed for many months that a peace settlement would occur between the two villages. Just weeks before their departure God allowed them to see the beginnings of His restoration.

There was a peace ceremony where leaders spoke and people from Kudjip and Konduk ate together, symbolizing their desire to forgive and quit the fighting. One great loss had been the closing of the Konduk church when the congregation scattered. Jim and Kathy were thrilled when they were able to attend the first service of this church's reopening in May, just weeks before they left the country. When they arrived back in PNG in 1995, they wrote:

> We have been to Konduk church three times and always enjoy it. The children have good memories there, which seem to overshadow the sad ones. There will be an official church reopening revival and baptism in a few weeks, which we will be involved in. Pray that it will be another part of the healing process toward real inner peace for these people who have fought and suffered for the fight.

The customs and traditions of PNG culture are deeply rooted in their tribal association. For centuries they have operated on the system of "payback" when a wrong is committed by one tribe against another. This has resulted in tribal war being used as a frequent method of settling disputes. Often the crime of one individual can cause an entire village to go into combat against another village with spears, bows and arrows, and axes. In the past several years there has been a marked change in the warfare as guns have become a part of the fighting equipment. (What a contrast this is to God's "payback" system celebrated in this book!)

Our Nazarene hospital has been in turmoil many times as tribes nearby engage in battles and bring their wounded for treatment. In some instances the hospital has had to close down for the safety of the nationals who are on staff, nursing students, and patients. These Papua New Guineans may be a part of a tribe that is being attacked and may be fearful of injury or involvement in the dispute.

In 1987 during a time of severe tribal unrest and local hostilities toward the hospital, the facility was closed for a full month. Missionaries are usually not endangered by the fighting and often have watched the battles from a safe distance, but occasionally there may be specific threats against a missionary or the hospital by a particular criminal, or "rascal" as they are called in PNG.

One of the anxieties we experience at home is for the safety of our family when there is tribal unrest. Usually, we find out about the dangers after the threat has subsided because the missionaries do not want to worry the relatives at home. We were surprised to hear that Jim slept with a baseball bat by his back door and an ax by his front door when the hospital had to close down. Even giving medical treatment to a person injured in tribal fighting could possibly be interpreted as the missionary doctor taking sides with a particular tribe.

This part of PNG culture, the tribal rivalry, is often the most difficult aspect for new Christian converts. Family loyalty is expected even when it means revenge or violence against others. Many times it is difficult for the Christian to resist the pressure from his clan to participate in the extracting of "payback" by committing crimes against a nearby village. As can be seen in the Kudjip/Konduk dispute, the fighting and hostility can last for many years.

Crime is a major sociological problem in PNG.

There is sometimes a lack of integrity or efficiency in the law-enforcement system of this developing country. Many times the "white skins" (foreigners) are victims of theft. They are seen as the "wealthy" in this third world country and are targeted by thieves as they go into town for shopping trips or travel the roads through the bush country. Many times someone is taken along to stand guard at the car while a missionary goes into stores to make purchases.

In 1987 the Radcliffes experienced a frightening robbery. They were returning home from a bush village and came upon a roadblock. Three masked gunmen held them up and took all of their possessions from the car. The rascals finished their mischief without harming the missionary family. Later the Radcliffes were able to recover some of the stolen goods, including new hiking boots Benjamin had just received from his grandma. The night they were robbed God brought comfort to them through the children's devotional book, which had this verse: "The eternal God is your refuge, and underneath are the everlasting arms" (Deuteronomy 33:27).

During the Radcliffes' second term they felt the need to have an alarm put on their doors because of the rash of break-ins on the mission station. They still found evidence one evening when they returned from church that a "rascal" had entered via their attic. Several things were missing, but the thief was not caught. Several months later as Jim was examining a patient, he solved the mystery when he noticed his JC Penney briefs being worn by this man. Here that would not be incriminating evidence, but in PNG very few men own JC Penney briefs.

Domestic violence is also severe in this country where polygamy is still common and legal. Dealing with multiple wives in the same family often results in much fighting and jealousy. Frequently the hospital has to treat trauma patients as a result of this particular problem. Not only do husbands abuse their wives, but sometimes angry wives will inflict serious injuries on their husbands or on another wife. On Christmas Eve of 1995 Jim did emergency surgery on a pregnant lady with a ruptured uterus whose husband had beaten her. She lost six units of blood, the baby, and her uterus as a result. Even though she recovered and her life was spared, this tragedy is too common and requires the power of God for deliverance.

Anyone who looks at tourist information or views pictures of Papua New Guineans usually sees colorful national costumes, painted faces, bright bird feathers, animal furs, beads, and seashells. This kind of festive clothing is called *bilas* and is only worn for special ceremonies. A few days after the Radcliffes left for the field in 1985, my three-year-old Katherine noticed a brochure with a photo of a tribal warrior in *bilas* on it. After realizing that this was from PNG, she asked, "Will Aunt Kathy and Uncle Jim paint their faces?"

Sometimes it is strange to think of my sister living in a place so different from the place I call

A Papua New Guinean in full festival dress.

home. Yet her experience with the Papua New Guinean culture has enriched me as well, and I like to think that, through my sister, I have a part of enriching the culture of PNG with the gospel as well.

4
The Lord Will Watch Over Your Coming and Going

THOSE WHO LIVE CLOSE to their extended families may have a hard time fully appreciating the blessing they have. Of course, to a family with missionaries, "close" is anything under 3,000 miles! Although our family likes to travel and had done quite a bit of it as we kids were growing up, traveling to the South Pacific would never have been a part of our family plans had the Radcliffes not lived in PNG. Those trips around the world were definitely motivated by our intense desire to see our loved ones.

Even though she had learned to cope with an occasional airplane trip in the United States, my mother surprised us all with her courage to make a trip to PNG. She had never been out of her home state until she was married and had to overcome a tremendous fear of flying during her young adult years. My youngest brother, Scott, graduated from high school in the spring of 1986 and decided his graduation present should be a trip to PNG. In June of that year, Mom and Scott joined a Work and Witness team from Indianapolis.

It was an expensive venture to send two family members on that project. Airfare alone to PNG is usually U.S.$1,700-2,000. Still, we considered that a small price to pay for some of us to have the chance to be with those we love.

During the visit of Kathy's mom and brother, we experienced our first loss in our family circle since the Radcliffes had gone to the field. Our Grandma Beam passed away on July 5, 1986, at age 88 after a brief hospital stay. In their newsletter Kathy wrote:

> We were saddened by a phone call from Dad Beam to tell of his mother's death while Mom and Scott were here. I was so sorry that we could not all be together there for Grandma's memorial service, but we know God's timing is right. To have my mother here was a special blessing. We had our own little memorial service and sang songs and shared special memories of her.

Every time a furlough ends and a missionary says good-bye to aging relatives it could be the last time, so these are especially difficult times. The hardest part for me personally was to have my father experience his mother's funeral without his life-companion here.

Even though I knew it would be a good thing for Kathy to have her mom there to share the burden of the loss, it was an unusually emotional time for us at home as we realized the limitations involved in the distance separating us. Making it home for a funeral isn't practical when the journey takes more than two days and costs thousands of dollars. The sharing of videotapes has become especially precious at these times. Several "homegoing celebrations" have been shared with the Radcliffes on video as four grandparents and some aunts and uncles have passed away during their terms in PNG.

The summer of 1986 also brought Jim's parents and his brother John for a visit to PNG. This was just one year after the Radcliffes arrived in PNG. Christmas of 1986 was the one time during their first term that Jim and Kathy came home. They took their vacation time and came to the States for two and a half weeks. It was a busy and stressful time for the entire extended family as we attempted to share the limited time not only with family members but with many friends who were eager to see the Radcliffes too.

In August of 1987 the Xenia, Ohio, Church of the Nazarene made a trip to PNG to build a church and housing for national workers near the hospital. My parents and my brother Dave were part of this team. They built a church in a remote village of Borona in just nine days, and it was dedicated to the memory of my grandmother who had passed away the year before.

The relationships built with the Papua New Guineans during those brief days were demonstrated by the farewell gifts they gave to the team members. Jim commented that some of them were giving items that cost them a significant percentage of their small income—gifts given lavishly from grateful hearts. What blessing was poured out upon those Work and Witness team members as they gave and received freely!

Within the first two years of mission work, Jim and Kathy had visits from all of their parents and three siblings. By this time I was the only member of my immediate family who had not been to PNG for a visit. When Kathy told us early in 1987 that she was expecting Radcliffe child number three, we began praying about the practicality of my own personal "work and witness" trip to help her when the baby came.

The finances, care of my own children, and uncertainty of timing made it a monumental decision. Finally, in September, the details seemed to come together to confirm that this "adventure of a lifetime" would come true for me and be blessed by the Lord. The gracious people of Regency Park Church in Tulsa gave generously to help with my expenses. God blessed me with a prosperous profit on a garage sale that fall too. My parents helped with finances as well, so I made arrangements for the three-week trip. My mother-in-law and mother shared the responsibility of caring for my own three young children, ages two, five, and eight.

Realizing the impossibility of predicting the arrival of a baby, we gambled on scheduling my arrival about two weeks before the due date. (Kathy's first two children arrived two to four weeks early, so we took that into consideration.) One can't book flights around the world at the last minute, and it would certainly be disappointing to make that trip and have the baby come after I came back home. So we just prayed for God's perfect timing and acted in faith. On November 14, two days before my scheduled departure, Kathy called to tell me that Timothy had just been born.

I left Tulsa, Oklahoma, at 2 P.M. on November 16, expecting to be in PNG in 36 hours. With a 6-hour delay on the first leg of my journey, I missed connecting flights and almost considered turning around and going back home because of the complications in my schedule. I had to stay in San Francisco overnight by myself. My 36-hour trip eventually stretched to four days with a 24-hour layover in Sydney, Australia.

As I struggled over releasing these unexpected inconveniences in my travel, I wrote in my journal:

> I trust that I will make it to New Guinea, but a day or so later! I commit my way to the Lord. Father, please go before me and help me to have wisdom in what questions to ask, how to reschedule my flights, phone calls to make, etc. I rest in the promise in Joshua 1:5 and 9 that You are with me: "I will never leave you nor forsake you. . . . Be strong and courageous. Do not be terrified; do not be discouraged, for the LORD your God will be with you wherever you go."

By the time I arrived, my new nephew was six days old. Many friends on the mission station had helped Kathy with meals during those first days, and now it was my turn to help. My prayer had been that we would be mutually encouraging to one another (see Romans 1:10-13); that there would be special moments of intimacy with each other as sisters that would center on God's grace and glory in our lives; that I would be not only a household helper but a helper in spirit to the entire Radcliffe household; and that God would give me a special love to express to each one of those five precious people, as well as to the nationals and missionaries that I met.

My welcoming committee was quite well prepared with a homemade sign for "Aunt Becky." I put in a request for a lei when I saw that lovely frangipani flowers used for these fragrant necklaces were growing in Kathy's yard! The missionary kids were accustomed to this craft.

There is simply no conceivable way to communicate the blessing of those sweet memories made during my time in PNG. The 10-page journal that I kept during my trip gives detailed accounts of every experience I had during those 13 days in PNG. Some highlights are included in this book, but each day held some deeply cherished fellowship with God's choice folks. Timothy's dedication and baby shower, a baptismal service and *mumu*, a trip into the "bush" area called the Jimi Valley, a Thanksgiving celebration, a Christmas concert, and lots of other good times were packed into those two weeks. God really did give me the "desire of my heart" and a richly rewarding time as I journeyed to the "far side of the sea."

It is hard to believe that all of those trips were packed into two and a half years of Jim's and Kathy's first term. Making visits at shorter intervals probably helped us all get used to the longer separations. The Radcliffes' newsletter discussed the importance of these visits to the Papua New Guineans. They said:

> We were overwhelmed by the love our PNG friends showed to our families. It was as if they wanted to express their gratitude to them for allowing their children and grandchildren to be here in their country. It really means so much to them to see that our family cared about Papua New Guineans. Our families received such blessings in return.

During the Radcliffes' second four-year term (1990-94) there was only one trip made to PNG. Helen Radcliffe went in July of 1992 when Radcliffe child number four was making her debut. Again we had to deal with the gamble of timing for a baby's arrival. Helen was going to be in PNG for 10 days, and Priscilla decided to join the world just 5 days before Helen came home again. Again God's timing was perfect and Grandma had half the time with her other three grandchildren and then got to spoil the newborn for a few days. Jim made an abbreviated trip to California by himself in October of 1990 for his brother John's wedding. God blessed that time by allowing the wedding date to coincide with a trip to a church conference that my husband and I were attending. My brother Scott and his new bride also lived in Pasadena at that time. So several of us experienced being together with Jim's family for the wedding that year.

The "Traveler's Psalm," Psalm 121, has been a chapter that has brought much comfort to me any time I have a journey ahead of me. It also applies to the many thousands of miles our family has traveled as we go east and west around the globe:

I lift up my eyes to the hills—
    where does my help come from?
My help comes from the LORD,
    the Maker of heaven and earth.
He will not let your foot slip—
    he who watches over you will not slumber;
indeed, he who watches over Israel
    will neither slumber nor sleep.
The LORD watches over you—
    the LORD is your shade at your right hand;
the sun will not harm you by day,
    nor the moon by night.
The LORD will keep you from all harm—
    he will watch over your life;
the LORD will watch over your coming and going
    both now and forevermore.

5

Strangers on Earth...

FURLOUGHS ARE DEFINITELY FULL of much "coming and going" for the missionaries. For many years all missionaries were on a five-year rotation with four years on the field and one year at home. Now there is much more variety in schedule, and missionaries have differing proportions of time at home and abroad.

Deputation services are a vital part of furlough as missionaries speak in churches and raise funds for their work. They also solicit prayer support, making Nazarenes aware of their specific needs on the field. One might assume that the furlough would be the favorite period of time for missionaries since they are coming "home." Although they do have happy reunions with friends and family, there are unique stresses to this experience that sometimes make it a difficult time.

Choosing a place to live is the first tough decision furloughing missionaries must make. Often they locate near relatives or have to move in with parents until a suitable house or apartment can be selected. (And we *all* know how stressful that can be if it lasts for more than a week or two.) Moving furniture across an ocean is usually not practical, so finding something furnished or accumulating used furnishings ("early attic" design) is often necessary. Sometimes the location for furlough is determined by the educational needs of the missionaries or their children. Several of our colleges and larger churches now have rental homes available for furloughing missionaries. What a blessing these places have been to many who have lived there!

The Radcliffes have spent both of their furlough years in Kathy's hometown of Xenia, Ohio. Jim's parents have pastored in Ohio, so they have been fairly nearby also. While on the mission field, their furniture has been stored with their parents so it is available for use when they rent a house for their furlough year.

The first furlough of 1989-90 started with the Radcliffes' arrival at the Columbus, Ohio, airport in early June. Even the planning and preparation for the welcoming committee can be emotionally stressful. I recall the dilemma of the family wanting to have those early moments together. But we all realize the tremendous compliment it is to have many others who have loved, prayed, and supported and who desire to be on the welcoming committee too. We have generally had lots of "extended family" or "adopted family" who accompany us to the airport. We usually locate a nearby McDonald's, which is the first place most MKs want to go when their feet hit United States soil. Here a large group can gather and mingle for an hour or so, allowing relaxed time for every person to greet the missionaries.

The airport scenes are always etched in our memories because of the intense emotion we all feel. We have laughed over one in particular. We were discussing who would get to hug Kathy first at the airport. I had taken the normal position of "firstborn boss" and was suggesting that Daddy *should* be first but I would be second. (I don't recall the logic of this arrangement. I think my mother wasn't in the competition because she wanted to get hold of the grandchildren first.) Well, Dad had the last laugh as Kathy came down the ramp from the plane and I lost all self-control, bolted out in front of everybody else, met her before she got to the end of the ramp, and got the first hug after all. Dad was just too slow!

Of course, half of the airport scenes are the poignant ones when furlough is over. The three farewells that we have experienced have been very different. The first one I described in a previous chapter as the Radcliffes departed in 1985. The second furlough ended in 1990 with eight children present at the airport. The oldest cousin was 11 and the youngest was 3. Even though they were more aware of the ensuing separation than the previous time, the cousins were not as emotional as the adults when it came to the good-byes.

The return to PNG in 1995, however, was an entirely new experience. We now had cousins ranging from age 16 years down to one week old. The adolescents all were acutely cognizant of how long four years would be. We didn't anticipate the added tears and emotional pain of the more mature cousins. Photos at the airport show lots of folks with red eyes and red faces.

The Radcliffes did a lot of deputation work during their first furlough in 1989-90 and found the travel to be very stressful, especially for the children (ages nine, six, and two). The contrast to their life on the field is monumental. In PNG their life is very simple with the small community on the mission station and very little travel, except for vacations and occasional weekend visits to churches in the "bush."

Now they were in the United States where many churches had been praying for them earnestly for four years. These congregations were eager to have personal contact with this family. It was often requested that the children come along for the services. So now the MKs were in the "fishbowl," having to hop in it every weekend and sometimes during the week. The children quickly became weary of this arrangement.

Jim and Kathy had to make decisions to bring balance to their family life and schedule that would ease the stress on all concerned. Often this meant separation for them as Jim would go and speak alone. Perhaps their own description would be the best—from their newsletter in May of 1990:

> We are nearing the end of a wonderful year, our first furlough. It has been a rich time of visiting in the homes and churches of relatives and friends. We feel so blessed to have been with our loved ones. The year flew by. At times we have wondered, "Where is home?"

But we have realized how much "at home" we were with God's people across the U.S.A.! We do feel like we are going back home as we prepare to return to PNG.

We felt the Lord helped us find a balance and enjoy variety in this very unusual year. The first months found us traveling together as a family. The grandmas each accompanied us on a long trip. After school started, we took each week at a time; sometimes Jim traveled alone, usually on weekdays for district tours; sometimes the entire family went together for a weekend; other times just Timothy went with Mommy and Daddy for long weekend trips while Ben and Bekah stayed with Grandma. The Lord has been faithful in every area of our lives as we traveled and shared in our services. He has filled the lonely times of separation and given us safety on the roads. It was a joy to be in Xenia, Ohio, and at our home church this year. The pastor and people have been very supportive and helpful.

We have felt God's presence and blessing in the deputation services as His Spirit has enabled us to speak and has moved among the congregations. We have rejoiced in the testimonies of spiritual and physical miracles in the lives of you, God's people in the U.S.A., just as we have felt you rejoice as we shared about Papua New Guinea miracles. The Lord has revealed to us that one of the main reasons He led us to do deputation work was so that He could raise up prayer support for God's work in PNG.

During their second furlough Jim desired to do medical work to update his surgical skills. It was also necessary for him to take comprehensive exams to be recertified by the American Board of Surgery. This limited his choices to a surgical practice that would allow him to work with them for only one year. With the cost of malpractice insurance being high and Jim's stay in the United States so brief, few medical colleagues would consider this a mutually desirable arrangement. We all just prayed for the Lord's perfect plan.

In 1984, the year before Jim left for Papua New Guinea, he had been part of a general surgery practice in Xenia. This group of surgeons offered him a one-year contract again in 1994. It was a fulfilling year of ministry to patients, and Jim learned a lot of new surgical skills. Often during this year Jim was encouraged by his medical friends to reconsider his return to PNG and stay on in Xenia. Many people in the medical profession have a difficult time understanding why a doctor would give up a medical career in the United States and go to a "developing" country. Jim still continued to pray with patients and witness to them about Jesus, just as he does in PNG. But the call to PNG remained clear. The rewards of seeing desperate needs for healing met in Jesus' name in a developing culture are greater than a six-digit annual income.

One of the biggest adjustments for missionary families during furlough is reverse culture shock, coming back to their own culture, which has changed so dramatically in their absence. During the Radcliffes' first term, they had a three-week visit to the States in the middle of their term. But there were no trips to the United States during their second term, and the differences were much more obvious.

Kathy recalls hearing veteran missionaries discuss furlough with some dread. As a first-term missionary she could not relate to their feelings. She could hardly wait to get "home." Her children were all very young during the first furlough, but by the time their second furlough occurred, there had been eight years of PNG enculturation. Her children were more Papua New Guinean than American by then!

The first few months of furlough in '94 were so much harder than the first furlough that Kathy could now relate to the "disadvantages" that she had heard discussed by more experienced missionaries. Now the whole family was more severely affected by the reverse culture shock. The children were older and more involved with the culture socially. How much more slow and complicated was the adjustment this time!

The moral decline in America was very obvious to Jim and Kathy. They were shocked that American Christians *weren't* shocked at much of anything. The complexity of lifestyle and the materialism were almost overwhelming for the first few months at "home." It was difficult for the entire extended family as we all sought to understand our differences culturally. They were more pronounced than we anticipated.

The most painful part of it all was feeling somewhat "distanced" from my sister simply because I could not totally relate to what she was experiencing. After waiting four long years to be "close" together again, it took a while to reestablish an intimate relationship where we discussed our true feelings. As the Radcliffes were ending furlough they said in a newsletter that they were "troubled by life in the U.S.A. at first, but later felt encouraged by revival in their church and by conferences like those of Promise Keepers and the Institute of Basic Life Principles." They expressed their desire for God to be calling families and individuals to stand firm for holiness in the United States.

There are many special memories to be made and crowded into one year when furlough comes around. One of the most special has been our Sisters' Retreat. Before the Radcliffes' first furlough I heard a woman mention that she and her sister went away together once a year. I filed that idea away for future reference when it would be possible for me to use it.

Our first retreat was at a bed and breakfast in southern Ohio in 1989. Kathy planned it because I was living in Oklahoma then. I came to Ohio for a long weekend with my three children. Grandma and Dr. Jim baby-sat while we retreated for about 24 hours nearby. We took a driving tour of covered bridges through the country in our home county. Our accommodations were quite luxurious and included a morning dip in a hot tub in the brisk autumn air. Late night discussions were a natural part of the experience. (Often our times together are with 10 to 15 other family members present. Consequently, long, intimate conversations are not possible or practical. Taking care of the meals and children generally consume our time when the entire clan is together.)

On the next furlough we had a unique retreat experience at a Roman Catholic monastery in middle Kentucky. Kathy came from Ohio, and I drove north from Tennessee to meet for a couple of days at the Abbey of Gethsemane. It is the home of Trappist monks who share their facilities with those who desire a place for solitude and spiritual reflection. One week each month is set aside for women to stay in the retreat center.

We had no idea what would be in store for us there but trusted it would be conducive to our desire for spiritual sharing, fellowship, and worship. We were not permitted to talk during meals in the dining room or in our bedrooms because of the required silence in these places. There were "visiting rooms" provided for quiet conversation, as well as lovely grounds to explore as we walked and talked. We took some personal time for resting, reading, and relaxing. My favorite times were our times of prayer together. This was a rich and fulfilling way to enhance our relationship as sisters.

Furlough year has many challenges and blessings for the faithful heroes we call missionaries. The writer to the Hebrews mentions his list of faith heroes and then describes them this way: "And they admitted that they were aliens and strangers on earth. People who say such things show that they are looking for a country of their own. If they had been thinking of the country they had left, they would have had opportunity to return. Instead, they were longing for a better country—a heavenly one. Therefore God is not ashamed to be called their God, for he has prepared a city for them" (Hebrews 11:13c-16).

Don't you think this passage could be descriptive of furloughing missionaries? As I watched my sister's family struggle for nearly half of their 12 months at home, feeling like "aliens and strangers" in their country of birth, I also saw the obvious faith of ones who are looking for a heavenly city to call home. God had carefully prepared for them an American city for that one year of furlough. It didn't seem like "home" at first, but the Lord gave grace to them until it did feel more comfortable. And besides, no place on earth is *really* home to one who belongs to heaven!

During their second furlough, Dr. Jim wrote an inspired paraphrase that includes many of his thoughts and feelings regarding that year. He shared this as he spoke in his deputation services. Jim suggested that a chapter on furloughs be included in this book and gave me his permission to include this reading.

A Missionary's Twenty-third Psalm
by Dr. James Radcliffe

The Lord is my shepherd, I will not worry about raising our financial support, for He knows our needs and has blessed our deputation offerings and services. He makes me to lie down in a nice house next door to the hospital where I have updated my surgery skills. He leads me beside the quiet waters of spiritual refreshment and renewal at our home church. He restores my soul, my sense of calling, my vision for the work, and my spiritual passion in this year of furlough. He guides me in paths of righteousness and holiness from God's Word as preached by our pastor and evangelists. How we long to be a sanctified family ready to see Jesus!

Even though I walk through the valley of danger in pagan America with unfriendly lawyers, satanism, New Age philosophy, secular humanism, and adverse insurance companies, I will fear no evil. Or on the mission field with angry warriors, tropical illnesses, unhappy villagers, greedy thieves, and jealous witch doctors, I will fear no evil. For Your rod and Your staff, Your prayer warriors and mighty angels, Your Holy Spirit's presence and friendship, Your Word, and my missionary coworkers, they comfort me.

You prepare many tables before me at Faith Promise banquets and Prayer and Fasting potlucks. With these and fast-food restaurants while on the road, free doughnuts at the hospital (not to mention Grandma's cooking), I have had to buy larger clothes. You anoint my head with lots of new medical knowledge, which, hopefully, will be useful to help our people in Papua New Guinea.

My cup of blessings overflows. The acts of generous kindness, love, concern, and friendship from friends, family, and our churches have been humbling and overwhelming at times. Surely goodness and love will follow me all the miles and days of our missionary journeys, and we will all dwell in heaven together with our brothers and sisters from Papua New Guinea because of your prayers and support.

6

Whatever Your Hand Finds to Do

SOME OF MY FAVORITE information from PNG comes from my brother-in-law, Dr. James Radcliffe, affectionately known by many in PNG and at home as "Dr. Jim." In all of their newsletters he gives reports of the highlights of his medical work. Even in our family correspondence we will hear of Jim's recent surgeries. Often the name of a patient will be shared with specific needs for us to lift to the Lord. We have a part in Jim's ministry as we hear the news of how God has worked as we have prayed.

Dr. Jim's medical ministry is full of great stories from his daily work in the Nazarene hospital at Kudjip. And everyone loves a good story. It would be impossible to tell all of them, but we'll choose a few.

Jim's first surgery was performed five days after he arrived at the mission. In an early correspondence Jim writes:

> The Lord has answered many prayers at

the "haus sik" (hospital or "house of the sick"). At first I felt overwhelmed by the number of patients to take care of and by the new and unfamiliar diseases. Now I do enjoy the work and have felt God's compassion for the sick and dying. I want to allow Jesus to flow through my hands, my touch, my heart, and my lips to those who need Him here. I feel fulfilled now knowing I am where God wants me and doing what He has prepared and called me to do.

Surgery has gone well despite my first patient dying postoperatively. God has been working in the "haus bilong katim" (operating room or "house where cuts belong"). I felt the Lord's help especially during my first C-section here since I had not seen one in five years. We felt it was providential that I spent 30 minutes the previous night reading about cesareans after talking with a missionary midwife about the obstetrical problems here!

The glory is always given to God for His intervention in the impossible cases. Many times God makes up the difference when there are difficult situations where equipment, medicines, or skills are lacking. Dr. Jim continually refers to the "bank" of prayers he relies on when an emergency arises in his work. As the saints are interceding for the medical work, these prayers are being stored like incense in golden bowls up in heaven to be drawn upon when the need arises (see Revelation 5:8).

Dr. Jim's real passion is for evangelism to occur in the hospital along with the medical treatment he administers. Prayer is a regular part of His ministry, and he often prays with patients to receive Jesus as Savior. There are hospital evangelism teams who visit each ward of the hospital regularly to hold brief services with singing and guitar music, scripture, and prayer. The chaplains reported 150 conversions at the hospital in 1995. Two new churches were started as patients who were converted returned to their village areas. Since the Radcliffes live right next door to the hospital, occasionally Kathy will make rounds with Jim just to be a part of his medical work and be more aware of his patients and their needs.

In the first months of Jim's work in the operating theater at Kudjip Nazarene Hospital, he operated on a 14-year-old boy named Masa. He was an innocent bystander when two tribes began throwing rocks, spears, and knives, and he was stabbed in the back. Masa had no blood pressure when he came to the emergency room and received six units of blood, including some from a missionary. He was rushed to surgery with a huge collection of blood in the back of his abdomen from a laceration to major vessels, and Jim had to remove a kidney. There was great concern since the only "life support" equipment in the hospital is some CPR equipment that sometimes works. There is no intensive care unit and no ventilators.

Masa was in a coma for three days and was unresponsive mentally for several more days from the shock. Three answers to prayer were a part of his miraculous recovery process. First, Dr. Jim stopped in the middle of surgery, because he feared that Masa would die, to ask for God's wisdom and skill to find the bleeding source. Second, the staff prayed for Masa to awaken from the coma, which was felt to be due to possible brain injury from the low blood pressure. Third, he later received Jesus into his heart as Lord and Savior. He gradually began talking, eating, and walking around after he regained consciousness. God spared his life so that he could glorify his Redeemer and Healer.

The successful recovery of patients who are injured in tribal fights is important to spare further fighting. Often tribal fighting is escalated as the "payback" system encourages revenge for injuries or deaths suffered by enemy lines. Such was the case with Masa's postoperative recovery. Both tribes were anxiously awaiting the final results of his trauma.

Masa gave his heart to the Lord soon after his surgery. He has maintained a close friendship with the Radcliffes through all these years. The Radcliffes wrote about him saying:

> His visits to our home are a blessing. Many times he has brought cabbage or fruit from his garden to share with us. Sometimes he comes just bearing a beautiful smile that radiates the love of Jesus and his gratitude for the place he finds himself today.

Since I prayed for Masa during his recovery, it was a personal delight for me to be able to meet him during my visit to PNG two years later. We were taking a ride to a nearby village for a picnic when we passed Masa walking along the dirt road. Jim stopped the car and introduced me to him. With a proud smile, Masa pulled up his shirt to show me the scar from his surgery.

During the Radcliffes' second term, Masa entered Bible school, graduated, and started a new church on the top of a mountain near their home. When they returned after their furlough year in 1995 to begin their third term, Masa was one of their first visitors and began to help them replant their garden. What joy it brings to see the maturity in these people whom God has allowed the hospital work to touch and change, both physically and spiritually! What a joy to share in that through my connection to the Radcliffes and through prayer!

In 1990 Jim wrote about an especially rewarding experience in his work:

> A boy named Paul was hit by a truck early one morning. He had severe, open fractures of both legs and one arm. We had to eventually amputate one leg. He has finally healed well and is in good spirits. He can walk with a walker. Paul has been in the hospital three months. On Christmas Day his old father, who is a village headman and a tribal fight leader, wanted to pray to ask Jesus into his heart for the first time. What a special Christmas present on rounds that day! That is why I enjoy being a medical missionary!

The Papua New Guineans often express gratitude to the relatives of missionaries for their support. Every time one of my family members has visited PNG, we have come home with gifts from the people there. There is a feeling of mutuality in this grateful spirit since we appreciate the love shown to the Radcliffes from the Papua New Guineans as well. Jim and Kathy's national pastor, Mundua, and his wife, Dorome, were very gracious to me as I fellowshipped with them when I went to PNG. His pastoral care for the Radcliffes has created a special place in my heart for them.

A letter in 1991 tells of the surgery Jim performed upon their pastor's wife at Kudjip. It is told from Kathy's perspective:

> The day before we left for our vacation, Dorome (Pastor Mundua's wife) had surgery for a ruptured ectopic pregnancy. During the surgery Jim came out and talked to her husband about doing a hysterectomy. The risk of another ectopic pregnancy was high, because her other tube was blocked. It was also unlikely that she would ever have a normal pregnancy.
>
> Pastor Mundua told Jim to do what he felt God would have him do. As we were standing by the window in the courtyard watching the surgery in the operating room, I shared with Mundua the message Jim had preached many times last year about the importance of prayer in our work here. It was so real to me that Jim needed the Lord's wisdom so many times in emergency situations.
>
> Mundua and Dorome have had beautiful testimonies through all of this. They had hoped for these 14 years of marriage to some-

time bear a child, yet they have seen God's hand in their lives, even as that hope died. Jim did do a hysterectomy, and Dorome has recovered well. I am wondering if they will adopt another child since their adopted daughter, Esther, is about 10 years old now.

A patient who had much influence in PNG for a few years was an AIDS patient named David. In 1991 Jim was chairman of the provincial AIDS committee. The disease is increasing, and efforts are being made to educate the public.

David had a dramatic conversion and became a tremendous witness for the Lord as part of Kudjip's AIDS team. This group traveled to high schools to present dramas and teaching about God's laws regarding sexuality and marriage. David impacted the lives of many young people even in the end stages of this terrible disease. He would say, "I am suffering the consequences of my sin, but I have hope because I have Jesus!"

David wanted to die in Kudjip Nazarene Hospital where he would be surrounded by Christians who loved him. He was a blessing to the hospital staff and many of his family members. David called his family together to ask forgiveness for his offenses against them before he told them good-bye. He went to be with his Jesus in 1992.

There is always an overwhelming response of generous Nazarenes when they know of the needs for rolled bandages, various medications, vitamins, and other hospital supplies. Because of the newly developed community-based health-care program being established, the list of needs is changing. Large quantities of basic medical supplies have been provided through Med-care Paks donated by churches in North America through NWMS. These have been and will be used by the community health volunteers in their villages to treat their own people.

In 1996, a shipment of Med-care Paks arrived containing soap, bandages, adhesive tape, thermometers, nonprescription medicines, cotton balls, and other basic items that most of us usually have stocked in our medicine cabinets—even safety pins and sealable bags! What a blessing will be "broken and spilled out" on Papua New Guineans as these gifts are given to them by their more prosperous Christian brothers and sisters from America!

There have been several times when Jim has done surgery on fellow missionaries or other expatriates because he is the only available one to do the operation in the area. The doctors and the Nazarene hospital and staff are well-respected throughout PNG and have been complimented highly on their work by government officials. The entire country only has about 50 hospitals. The Nazarene hospital has the reputation for being one of the finest, even though some would count it inadequate in comparison to some western medical facilities.

As important as the hospital is to the ministry of the Church of the Nazarene in PNG, the emphasis has shifted in our medical work to reaching out with primary health care and village training. In 1995 a field study was conducted by general church leaders, missionaries, and nationals regarding the future of the PNG medical work. The results confirmed the need to continue the hospital work, including surgery, and to increase the efforts in preventive health care in village areas. The focus was to empower the people of PNG to make decisions regarding their health needs.

A present focus of our Nazarene medical work has been to build "health centers" in outlying areas and staff these with a medical person, not necessarily a doctor. Centers have been opened in Sangapi and Imane in recent years. Dr. Jim and family will occasionally go to visit these health centers, and he will treat people while they are visiting.

Many government health centers exist throughout the country, and our Nazarene doctors have been asked to visit these clinics "in the bush" as well. During my visit to PNG in 1987, Jim visited two clinics at Tabibuga and Nondugl. I saw a man with leprosy and a woman with a football-sized tumor on her neck at those clinics and realized once again the tremendous physical needs of these people.

Dr. Jim commented, "We really need the Lord's wisdom and more understanding of the culture as we launch out in this area of preventative medicine." With education in sanitation and some health-care basics, many illnesses that bring Papua New Guineans to the hospital can be prevented. That is especially important when you consider that many village people have to walk for two days to reach Kudjip for treatment.

Still, for now at least, the ministry of the hospital is very important in PNG. And as with any ministry, there are always needs. One remarkable answer to the needs of the hospital has been the installation of a hydroelectric plant, almost fully financed by a group of European businessmen. In a recent newsletter PNG missionaries Marvin and Patti Thrasher report:

> Thank you for all your prayers these past two years as we finished the new hydroelectric plant. When we returned in June 1994, we had what seemed to be an insurmountable amount of work to do in order to finish the hydro. But each week we were able to move ahead, and we finished the work in late 1995. In the middle of February just past (1996), we had the engineer who designed the hydro, Mike Johnson of Indonesia and Washington State, complete the final installation of the generator, governor, and the computer system that controls the whole thing. The hydro is producing about 150 kilowatts of power and the fuel is free, for we get many more gallons of fuel each day as it continues to rain more than usual (about 16 feet a year). The new hydro will save your hospital about K66,000 a year or U.S. $50,000.

When Jim first went to Kudjip, the idea of a surgeon was new and, to some, impractical. The hospital is always so overcrowded with general medical needs that it seemed to increase the work load to have a doctor taken out of the outpatient clinic to do surgery. The need for an anesthetist and other costly equipment in the operating room made it seem financially difficult. Jim had been advised during his training not to specialize in surgery because of this, but he felt definitely called of God to do surgery and trusted Him for the future.

When Jim came in 1985, the compromise was to schedule surgery only one day per week at first. Other emergency surgeries could be done as well. God has provided so beautifully for the needs of a smooth-functioning operating room. Anesthetist Jan Watson, missionary from Australia, has been a faithful and efficient person in the OR for eight years. A nationally trained nurse anesthetist now efficiently gives anesthesia so that Dr. Jim can operate. The scrub nurses have been Papua New Guineans.

The training of these national nurses has been a challenge and then a blessing as they have grown in their skill and effectiveness. Dr. Jim is pleased when his scrub nurse anticipates what surgical instrument to put in his hand before he asks. Jim says, "What a joy is it to work with skilled, committed, and spiritually concerned Christian staff who carry a burden for the patients!"

Currently the hospital schedules surgery four days per week. The surgery schedule consists of major surgeries on Tuesday and Thursday, minor surgery on Wednesday, and scopes and procedures on Friday. Two or three times per week the need arises for emergency surgery. What a blessing it is to have this available, especially when a life can be saved!

Another area of medical work that is very vital to the hospital is that of volunteer doctors coming to help. Often medical students come to experience part of their education at Kudjip for a few months. When the furlough schedule of the regular missionary doctors causes them to be short-staffed, many times a volunteer is able to fill in the gaps and provide relief for the overload of work. Usually there are four or five missionary doctors working at Kudjip. The Radcliffes enjoy the visits of these students and volunteers and often find great satisfaction in sharing their lives and work with these important visitors.

One of Dr. Jim's medical stories is my favorite because I was present too. We will title this one "Surgery Observed" (and if you're the squeamish type, you might want to skip this part).

The operating room in our Nazarene hospital in PNG is "open to the public" via a large window. Family members can stand outside in a courtyard and observe as much of the operation as they wish. Because laws are not as strict as in other countries, Jim was legally able to invite me right into the surgery theater when I made my visit in 1987, an opportunity I would have missed had Jim been practicing in the United States.

He was scheduled to do an abdominal surgery on a woman who was suffering from an obstruction. Jim's assistant that day was a visiting Nazarene obstetrician from the United States. The guest doctor's wife was observing surgery with me. We put on our green "scrubs" as the doctors were preparing themselves. Dr. Jim asked me how long we planned to stay. My answer was rather vague: "I don't know. It depends on how well I handle seeing all of this!" I had my video camera along to prove I really did it!

The initial abdominal incision didn't cause me to faint, and I was in awe of the procedure as I watched the surgeon work. Dr. Jim was pulling the large intestine out and then going over it manually section by section. As he cleaned a length of the intestine, he would then place it upon the patient's chest and move on to the next part. After awhile the pile was getting fairly large. I was fascinated by how much was inside that little woman.

Finally, I whispered a question to the doctor's wife observing beside me, "Do you suppose all that has to be put back in a certain order?" No sooner had the words come out of my mouth than I saw the doctor push the pile of intestines with one big "plop" right back into her abdomen. I guess that answered my question. No wonder people are sore after surgery!

During Jim's deputation tour in 1994-95, he told the story of an unusual series of surgeries that he had done shortly before his return to the States. An infant was born without a rectal opening. He knew it was urgent to do something to preserve the baby's life, but he had never done this surgery. He pulled out medical books and read about the required repair-surgery. Jim says he literally did this surgery with the textbook open in the operating room.

After the child's second surgery, the boy, who by that time had been named "Jim," had a postoperative complication. Dr. Jim prayed for God's wisdom and guidance and prayed with the distraught family. God again answered prayer, and the boy recovered. Just before Dr. Jim's furlough, he performed a third surgery. After that, "Little Jim's" mother and his father, a village chief, gave their hearts to Christ.

One of the ways people in Papua New Guinea honor those they love and respect is to name their children after them. It has been the privilege of many missionaries to have national Papua New Guineans share their first name. There are actually four little "Jims" in PNG who are Dr. Jim's namesakes. One is Masa's son (Jim's surgical patient mentioned earlier). Another is the boy with the serious birth defect that was just described. Another woman named her son after Jim since he delivered her baby by C-section. Bringing healing to the precious children of Papua New Guinea must be a rewarding experience. Sometimes Dr. Jim receives thoughtful gifts from these grateful families such as hand carvings, paintings, vegetables, and fruit from their gardens.

I am a pianist and often reflect on how blessed I am to have hands that can work and do as I have trained them! This applies equally to the skill needed by a surgeon. Our congregation sings a chorus that says, "These are holy hands. He's given us holy hands. He works through these hands and so these hands are holy."

We take for granted the ability many of us have to use our hands for ministering Christ's love, whether it be through a surgical procedure, manual assistance for a bedridden patient, a keyboard played, a letter typed, a handshake, a wave, a back rub, a foot massage, a soft "tweak" on the cheek, pat on the back, or typing a book about missions as I am doing now.

Our families, church friends, neighbors, and even strangers can be blessed as we consider our hands instruments for loving for Jesus' sake. "Whatever your hand finds to do, do it with all your might" (Ecclesiastes 9:10). "Whatever you do, work at it with all your heart, as working for the Lord, not for men" (Colossians 3:23).

"This Pair of Hands" was written in 1963 as a tribute to a Nazarene missionary doctor, Howard Hamlin. I include the lyrics here to honor all who use their hands to glorify the Lord they love, especially Christian doctors and, particularly, Dr. James David Radcliffe.

These hands I give to thee, my Blessed Savior,
To do Thy will whatever love demands;
Redeemed and sanctified and in Thy favor,
I gladly yield to Thee this pair of hands.
To point the lost of earth to Calvary,
To lift the Cross that dying souls may see,
To bring Thy healing touch to darkest lands,
I give to Thee, my God, this pair of hands.*

---

*© 1963. Renewed 1991 by Lillenas Publishing Co. All rights reserved. Used by special permission. Words and music by Floyd Hawkins.

7

Whoever Does the Will of My Father...

MY SISTER AND I are just a couple of "home town girls" who lived in the same small rural community for the first 18 years of our lives. We are "Midwest farmer's daughters" who made our first significant geographical move when we went to college. Therefore, we found much security in the familiar surroundings and people we had always known. Our grandparents (both sets) were our only baby-sitters when our parents had to be gone. Our mother has often told us how difficult it was for her to let us go off to camp for a week, but she encouraged our independence and social development.

As a young child, Kathy was shy and often hesitant to spend the night with a friend. She was a meek and gentle girl with a somewhat timorous nature, so it came as a surprise to all of us when she was called to a lifetime commitment of being so far away from home.

God had prepared our mother's heart for her children to be released for specific service for the

Kingdom. He had revealed to her that one of her children had a special calling. This was quite some time before she heard Kathy testify to her call to missionary work. So the moment of revelation of Kathy's calling was a very exciting time for Mom spiritually. She was ready to give her child, whichever one it was, for whatever use God designed. Kathy's testimony was a confirmation of God's work in her child's life.

As I found my companion and married in 1974, it became obvious that my choices would include living far away from family also. When I first fell in love with a ministerial student, I resigned myself to the possibility of never living near my parents. This made it a special surprise when one year after our marriage we moved to an assignment just 30 minutes from my hometown. The gracious Lord allowed me to have my first child with grandparents near enough to baby-sit!

When my new son, Brannon, was nearly two years old, we moved to a church that was three hours away. I was struggling with this change of location when God allowed me to find Matthew 12:46-50: "While Jesus was still talking to the crowd, his mother and brothers stood outside, wanting to speak to him. Someone told him, 'Your mother and brothers are standing outside, wanting to speak to you.' He replied to him, 'Who is my mother, and who are my brothers?' Pointing to his disciples, he said, 'Here are my mother and my brothers. For whoever does the will of my Father in heaven is my brother and sister and mother.'"

What a precious truth! I still get blessed when I think of how rich I felt as I realized how many relatives I would have. As I adopted individuals from each congregation we pastored—sisters and brothers, parents and grandparents, aunts and uncles and cousins—I would never be without family. Jesus almost sounds disrespectful of His family here. But I believe He just was using the opportunity to teach again and went on out to visit His mom and brothers as soon as He made His point.

This passage became especially meaningful as the Radcliffes made their move to PNG. I knew that God would provide substitute family members for them, as He had for me. Just as I have experienced God's family substituting for relatives who are geographically distant, so the Radcliffes have found "family" on the mission field.

Around the world, holidays are times when all the missionary families together plan many special events to celebrate as if it were family reunion time. Back home, we are very grateful for those who take our place during those moments that can be especially lonely. Holidays are some of the most difficult times, and wishing for the presence of our extended family is inevitable. But all of us have found the holidays to be bearable as we allow God to fill the emptiness left by distant family members.

Among missionaries around the world it is customary that all adult missionaries affectionately become "aunt" ("auntie") or "uncle" to every MK. Jim and Kathy's children have many aunties and uncles in PNG, and they have, in turn, been auntie and uncle to other MKs. This special adoption runs deep in their hearts. We thank God for these special relationships and the need that is met through their love. One time after the children had done a musical performance, Kathy said that the aunties and uncles all acted like proud grandparents.

Some families include single missionaries in their holiday or birthday celebrations. Three-year-old Rebekah (and her mommy) reported about her birthday party: "Some of my special 'aunties' and 'uncles' came for lunch. You should have seen the Cabbage Patch cake that 'Auntie Barbara' made for me."

The first relationships to blossom are those among the missionary family, which is quite a large group at Kudjip mission station (about 40 to 50 people). Naturally, there are age factors, common interests, and specific work relationships that cause particular closeness among the missionaries. When Jim arrived, he was one of two doctors on the hospital staff with a third one coming three months later. These three couples spent quite a bit of time together and were all "new" missionaries.

When the Radcliffes first moved to Kudjip there was only one other missionary family with children. Their three children, plus many Papua New Guinean children, became Benjamin and Rebekah's playmates. Through the next several years more families with children were assigned to Kudjip. Each Radcliffe child has had special friendships both with peers and with numerous substitute relatives. Still, the missionary family is in a constant state of change as furlough years come and go, and it seems that "welcome" and "farewell" gatherings are the most common social events.

By 1992 there were enough MKs to organize a "one room school" that enrolled 12 students in grades one through eight. The Nazarenes in Volunteer Service (NIVS) program has been providing a teacher for each school year. Prior to this, MKs attended international schools in other nearby towns or were home-schooled.

High school students currently use one of two options. In the past they usually moved to a home called the Nazarene Hostel at the Wycliffe base at Ukarumpa. This home is managed by a missionary couple called house parents. At Ukarumpa there is a high school with many MKs from a variety of mission organizations. This boarding school is a five-hour drive from Kudjip, and teaching is done by Wycliffe missionaries. More recently, the high school students are doing individual studies at home, using videotapes of class sessions from a Christian high school in the United States.

The missionaries from more remote areas come to Kudjip for meetings several times a year and develop friendships through this association. They may have few or no other missionaries where they are assigned. On other occasions, missionaries and visitors to Kudjip take trips to the bush to visit their missionary colleagues. This describes the special relationship between the Radcliffes and the Vern Ward family. Vern and Natalie lived in the bush area of Dusin, which was accessible only by plane.

Benjamin and Rebekah have even flown in a small Mission Aviation Fellowship plane to spend several nights with their dear MK friends at beautiful Dusin, one of their favorite spots in PNG.

Often special relationships develop across denominational lines as Nazarenes become friends with other missionaries and visit them for a "holiday" weekend. The Radcliffe family has made many special memories visiting the Swiss mission station at Mondomil. Two dear single ladies were missionaries there. These sisters, Dora and Christine Mattman, became very special friends to Jim and Kathy through their visits. Dora later died at the Nazarene hospital after a massive heart attack during the Radcliffes' second term.

Of all the special relationships that have grown out of Kathy's first two terms in PNG, one of the most intimate ones was with her special friend and prayer partner, Evelyn Wiens. She was better known as "Ev," or "Auntie Ev" to the children. Ev is a nurse from Canada and had some years of service in Africa before her assignment to PNG in 1985.

During the Radcliffes' first year in PNG, Ev would often stop by for visits with Kathy on her way to or from work since the hospital is next door to their home. Before long a very close relationship developed where Aunt Ev was included in many birthday and holiday celebrations at the Radcliffes' home.

In 1988 I received a special "thank you" letter from Ev for sharing my sister with her. She was es-

Evelyn Wiens with young Priscilla Radcliffe.

pecially close to my nephew, Timmy, who was one year old by then. Ev had been present at Timmy's birth, and I had come to PNG when he was six days old. She was reflecting on the first year of Timmy's life and said:

> As an adult I've never been close enough to a friend or relative with a baby where I've been able to see the daily changes and development that occur during the first year of a child's life. You have no idea what a blessing it has been to me to share in the joy of watching Timothy grow during this past year. I love Ben-

ji and Bekah so very much too. But seeing Timothy respond to me with love when he can't say it verbally has blessed me to pieces!

Ev had become involved in a new ministry of teaching primary health care in the villages during her 1990-94 term. This took her away from Kudjip mission station for overnight visits in the bush. Even though her work was productive and fulfilling, it was stressful for her. On February 4, 1994, she was found comatose in her apartment at Kudjip and taken to Australia by emergency plane.

There were many days and weeks of changing diagnoses and varied analyses regarding the cause of her collapse and subsequent slow improvement. The missionaries and nationals in PNG felt a great loss as they experienced the absence of Ev's kind ways and sweet spirit. The uncertainties and difficulties as she was unresponsive to medical attention caused them to spend more time in prayer and spiritual warfare. Ev had been praying for revival in PNG at any cost. Her intense desire for the Lord was evident as she memorized scripture and shared the Word with others. Kathy wrote home during these struggles:

> I am not sure exactly how the Lord is going to use this in all of our lives, but I do feel that we will realize God really loves and cares for Ev, that He is a God who answers prayer, that His ways are above our ways, and that He is being glorified and will continue to be glorified, not only in Ev's life, but also in many other situations, decisions, and heartaches that we

are facing. I feel that Ev's illness has brought me to know the Lord in a way I have never before known Him through prayer, fasting, and memorizing scripture. My own Bible study has been powerful and personal. The Lord has asked me to set aside my own agenda most days and called me to prayer. I have felt that the Lord is wanting me to gain an eternal perspective and to think about how we would live if He were to return for His own today.

This influence from Evelyn's life seemed to permeate the lives of many missionary colleagues and nationals as well.

Evelyn remained hospitalized in Australia with two Nazarene missionary nurses at her side daily for many weeks. Five months later, she returned to Canada for continued evaluation and treatment in a health-care center near her brother's home. Progress has been extremely slow, but Nazarenes around the world have prayed and continue to hope for Ev's improved health. The Radcliffes have been able to visit Evelyn once in Australia and twice in Canada during furlough.

The effect of her conscientious work in the villages is continuing to reap results. She is often mentioned and missed in the thriving primary health care work that she started in 1990. Carolyn Myatt, who spent 30 years in India in Nazarene medical work, moved to PNG in 1994 and has carried on the ministry Ev started in community-based health care.

The Radcliffes honored Ev by dedicating their

deputation slide presentation to her as they spoke in churches during furlough. Many of the pictures had been taken by Ev in preparation for her own furlough in 1994, which coincided with the Radcliffes' return home.

As can be seen, there was a great personal closeness between Evelyn and the Radcliffe family. This relationship existed for most of two terms, so her illness and subsequent departure from the mission station were a great loss to the Radcliffe family. They have had intense emotional pain as they have grieved the loss of this "neighbor" and "auntie." The hard unanswered questions about the causes and the future are still being given into the hands of our loving Lord. Evelyn's deep desire was that the Lord be glorified in her life.

A few days after the onset of Ev's illness Kathy found assurance from these words in John 11:4. "Jesus said, 'This sickness will not end in death. No, it is for God's glory so that God's Son may be glorified through it.'" Although there are no simplistic answers to this kind of suffering, many have already reaped the blessings of being touched by Evelyn Wiens's life and commitment to her Lord.

The people of Papua New Guinea have become precious to our family as they have been such dear friends and a vital part of the Radcliffes' lives. Both Jim and Kathy have emphasized their deep commitment to develop intimate relationships with the people of Papua New Guinea. It seems they have personified 1 Thessalonians 2:8: "We loved you so much that we were delighted to share with you not only the gospel of God but our lives as well, because you had become so dear to us."

You might expect that Jim's work would be the primary source of involvement with the nationals, but this is not so. All of their lives have been given to be used in numerous ways to evangelize and disciple these people.

Kathy has had many Papua New Guineans in her home, both in large groups and as individuals and families. Her early ministry was called "Pikinini Club" and was a weekly children's meeting in her home. She also had a biweekly ladies' meeting called "Meri Bung" where PNG women would share in the Word and prayer and discuss the joys and burdens of their lives. In 1993 she was involved in "Women of the Word" Bible studies with the women of the area. They often invite the Papua New Guineans to share in some of their holiday and birthday celebrations along with their fellow missionaries.

Discipling marriages has also become a vital ministry for Jim and Kathy. They held classes for those on the hospital staff, teaching Christian marriage principles. Jim has a vision for discipling young doctors and medical students to teach them surgery and soul winning.

Being pastored by a Papua New Guinea pastor has been very significant to the Radcliffes. The shepherd of the Pidgin congregation at Kudjip was Pastor Mundua during their first term. In 1992 this pastor was leaving PNG to go to Asia-Pacific Nazarene Theological Seminary in Manila, Philippines.

As the Radcliffes grieved over the emotional farewells to Pastor Mundua, his wife, Dorome, and daughter, Esther, Kathy recounted the following in their newsletter:

> Cultural barriers have not hindered his sensitivity to our needs. He came to our home, shared God's Word, and prayed with us when we returned home after being held at gunpoint on the road in 1986; when we received a phone call informing us that Kathy's mother had unexpected surgery for cancer (Mom is healed and well today); and when we were in turmoil over the fighting that occurred in our village during language study. Each time the Lord used Mundua in a powerful way to speak peace and comfort to us. Mundua also was the one who dedicated Timothy to the Lord when he was a newborn.

The verses Mundua shared that spoke peace after the robbery were Psalm 9:9-10. "The LORD is a refuge for the oppressed, a stronghold in times of trouble. Those who know your name will trust in you, for you, LORD, have never forsaken those who seek you." It had not been common for a national pastor to "call" upon a missionary in their home, but a cultural bridge was erected as the Radcliffes experienced some real needs.

Another pastor who has developed a close relationship with the Radcliffes is the pastor of the Konduk church, Pastor Peter. As the Radcliffes prepared to live in that village in 1991 for language study, they became very involved in the life of that congregation. As they made plans to live "in the bush" for six months, it was because of their intense desire to bridge the cultural gaps. This would increase their understanding of the culture, thereby making them more effective in their ministry. Pastor Peter was their close neighbor, ate many meals with them, and helped them with their language. As the tribal fighting destroyed the village and dispersed his flock in October of 1991, the Radcliffes shared in his sorrow. The next year, when Priscilla was born, Pastor Peter participated in her dedication ceremony.

Often the way we as a missionary's family make our initial acquaintance with the people of PNG who are friends of Radcliffes is through video. Papua New Guineans love to be photographed, even though they are typically a timid people. Jim and Kathy often attempt to "interview" them for us, and they are more likely to just smile and giggle. Sometimes they will say a few words in Pidgin English and the Radcliffes will translate the message for us. We enjoy meeting many people this way whom we have never met face-to-face.

A large percentage of the friendships with Papua New Guineans results from hospital contacts through Jim's work. Nurses, nursing students, and other hospital staff members have become very dear to Dr. Jim and his family. It was a special treat for us to be able to meet some of these friends who were delegates from PNG to the General Assembly in 1993 in Indianapolis. Since Jim and Kathy weren't there, we delivered greetings and hugs via these precious national people as they returned to PNG.

An international family has developed for the Radcliffes in PNG. People of many different nationalities besides American are serving in this country. And we at home have all been blessed with a rich experience as our missionary loved ones have found true brothers and sisters in all of these choice servants of God's kingdom. There is no possible way to mention every person.

"And everyone who has left houses or brothers or sisters or father or mother or children or fields for my sake will receive a hundred times as much and will inherit eternal life" (Matthew 19:29). These words assure us that God's payback system is incredible! All our spending He will repay.

EPILOGUE

*Good measure, pressed down,
shaken together, running over . . .*

IN JUNE OF 1996 Kathy's and my father, Marvin Beam, received a serious and shocking diagnosis of cancer of the kidney and liver. We called the Radcliffes in PNG and then faxed the doctor's report to Dr. Jim. Suddenly the distance and separation were more painful than ever before.

The next day I asked the Lord to give us something to help us smile. A phone call from PNG that very morning resulted in many smiles—Josiah Daniel Radcliffe made his debut on June 18. Within 24 hours, Dr. Jim completed the baby's visa application and began to plan a trip home for August so my daddy could see his new grandson. This decision indicated the gravity of Dad's prognosis, although we had been hesitant to ask the oncologist for details.

With our favorite doctor in PNG, we struggled to make decisions about treatment options. It was difficult to be satisfied with weekly phone calls or faxes when we wanted to be in constant communication. Dad's cancerous kidney was removed 10 days later, but we were disappointed to learn that the cancer had spread.

I spent my summer making weekly trips from

Tennessee to Ohio to be with my parents. I began to see the body of Christ from a new perspective. Our family had never experienced such a time of suffering, and we were in need of support and encouragement. I had no idea how extravagant God could be through His people.

My father had been a great churchman, a faithful Nazarene since 1950. He was an example of loyalty and love in his local church. He was a leader on the Southwestern Ohio District, serving on the Advisory Board for 30 years and attending General Conventions as a delegate since 1964. My parents had literally given their lives to the church. Now they began to reap untold rewards in a very practical sense.

The mail was a bright spot each day as scores of cards arrived. Several times a new $100 bill was included in a card or sent anonymously. A landowner who had rented farm acreage to Dad for 50 years canceled the $3,000 payment due in June. Friends started bringing food to the house the week of the diagnosis, and that continued throughout the summer.

When the Radcliffes arrived in August, the ladies from our home church planned and provided three meals a day for all 22 of us for an entire week. They continued to bring an abundance of food during the entire two months that the Radcliffes were home.

When people learned that the trip home from PNG for the entire Radcliffe family would cost more than $9,000, the demonstration of love was unbelievable. Nazarenes at our local church and at the Southwestern Ohio District NWMS Convention gave enough to pay the airfare. Relatives and friends outside of our community and church gave hundreds of dollars. Physicians in Xenia who had gotten to know Dr. Jim during his year of furlough gave generous gifts too.

Three days after the Radcliffes arrived home, Dad was so ill with the side effects of his first chemotherapy treatment that he was admitted to the hospital. It was a great comfort to have Dr. Jim, Kathy, and their children present during the four weeks of his hospital stay. When their three-week vacation ended, they were granted a short leave of absence. This was only made possible financially because of the generous gifts they had received. After 18 days of hospice care at home, Dad went to heaven on September 28, just 102 days after diagnosis.

In addition to the overwhelming displays of support throughout Dad's illness, we were even more humbled by the loving responses and comforting expressions extended after his death. Jesus has repaid us in unimaginable ways as we have walked through the valley of the shadow of death. Of course, none of this was a surprise to Him; He went before us to light the way.

We continue to be amazed by our great church. We have written hundreds of thank-you notes for the loving ways we have been remembered. But sometimes, even for this author, words just do not seem adequate. Once again God has "outdone himself." Luke 6:38 is true: "Give, and it will be given to you. A good measure, pressed down, shaken together and running over, will be poured into your lap." It really is true: "All thou spendest, Jesus will repay."